Twinsology Trivia Challenge

Minnesota Twins Baseball

Twinsology Trivia Challenge

Minnesota Twins Baseball

Researched by Ann E. Wilson

Paul F. Wilson & Tom P. Rippey III, Editors

Kick The Ball, Ltd

Lewis Center, Ohio

Trivia by Kick The Ball, Ltd

College Football Trivia

Alabama Crimson Tide	Auburn Tigers	Boston College Eagles	Florida Gators
Georgia Bulldogs	LSU Tigers	Miami Hurricanes	Michigan Wolverines
Nebraska Cornhuskers	Notre Dame Fighting Irish	Ohio State Buckeyes	Oklahoma Sooners
Oregon Ducks	Penn State Nittany Lions	Southern Cal Trojans	Texas Longhorns

Pro Football Trivia

Arizona Cardinals	Buffalo Bills	Chicago Bears	Cleveland Browns
Denver Broncos	Green Bay Packers	Indianapolis Colts	Kansas City Chiefs
Minnesota Vikings	New England Patriots	New Orleans Saints	New York Giants
New York Jets	Oakland Raiders	Philadelphia Eagles	Pittsburgh Steelers
San Francisco 49ers	Washington Redskins		

Pro Baseball Trivia

Baltimore Orioles	Boston Red Sox	Chicago Cubs	Chicago White Sox
Cincinnati Reds	Detroit Tigers	Houston Astros	Los Angeles Dodgers
Milwaukee Brewers	Minnesota Twins	New York Mets	New York Yankees
Philadelphia Phillies	Saint Louis Cardinals	San Francisco Giants	

College Basketball Trivia

Duke Blue Devils	Georgetown Hoyas	Indiana Hoosiers	Kansas Jayhawks
Kentucky Wildcats	Maryland Terrapins	Michigan State Spartans	North Carolina Tar Heels
Syracuse Orange	UConn Huskies	UCLA Bruins	

Pro Basketball Trivia

Boston Celtics	Chicago Bulls	Detroit Pistons	Los Angeles Lakers
Utah Jazz			

Visit **www.TriviaGameBooks.com** for more details.

For Paul Wilson,
Sonny & Dixie Richardson,
Billie Collins,
Sam, Leah, & William Richardson,
David & Ruby Richardson and Javier Castillo

**Twinsology Trivia Challenge: Minnesota Twins Baseball;
First Edition 2011**

Published by
Kick The Ball, Ltd
8595 Columbus Pike, Suite 197
Lewis Center, OH 43035
www.TriviaGameBooks.com

Edited by: Paul F. Wilson & Tom P. Rippey III
Copy Edited by: Ashley Thomas Memory
Designed and Formatted by: Paul F. Wilson
Researched by: Ann E. Wilson

For information on ordering this book in bulk at reduced prices, please email us at pfwilson@triviagamebooks.com.

International Standard Book Number: 978-1-934372-95-1
Printed and Bound in the United States of America
10 9 8 7 6 5 4 3 2 1

Table of Contents

Dear Friend,

Thank you for purchasing our *Twinsology Trivia Challenge* game book!

We have made every attempt to verify the accuracy of the questions and answers contained in this book. However it is still possible that from time to time an error has been made by us or our researchers. In the event you find a question or answer that is questionable or inaccurate, we ask for your understanding and thank you for bringing it to our attention so we may improve future editions of this book. Please email us at tprippey@triviagamebooks.com with those observations and comments.

Have fun playing *Twinsology Trivia Challenge*!

Paul & Tom

Paul Wilson and Tom Rippey
Co-Founders, Kick The Ball, Ltd

PS – You can discover more about all of our current trivia game books by visiting www.TriviaGameBooks.com.

Book Format:

There are four quarters, each made up of fifty questions. Each quarter's questions have assigned point values. Questions are designed to get progressively more difficult as you proceed through each quarter, as well as through the book itself. Most questions are in a four-option multiple-choice format so that you will at least have a 25% chance of getting a correct answer for some of the more challenging questions.

We have even added extra innings in the event of a tie, or just in case you want to keep playing a little longer.

Game Options:

One Player -
To play on your own, simply answer each of the questions in all the quarters, and in the overtime section, if you'd like. Use the Player / Team Score Sheet to record your answers and the quarter Answer Keys to check your answers. Calculate each quarter's points and the total for the game at the bottom of the Player / Team Score Sheet to determine your final score.

Two or More Players –
To play with multiple players decide if you will all be competing with each other individually, or if you will form and play as teams. Each player / team will then have its own Player / Team Score Sheet to record its answer. You can use the quarter Answer Keys to check your answers and to calculate your final scores.

The Player / Team Score Sheets have been designed so that each team can answer all questions or you can divide the questions up in any combination you would prefer. For example, you may want to alternate questions if two players are playing or answer every third question for three players, etc. In any case, simply record your response to your questions in the corresponding quarter and question number on the Player / Team Score Sheet.

A winner will be determined by multiplying the total number of correct answers for each quarter by the point value per quarter, then adding together the final total for all quarters combined. Play the game again and again by alternating the questions that your team is assigned so that you will answer a different set of questions each time you play.

You Create the Game -
There are countless other ways of using *Twinsology Trivia Challenge* questions. It is limited only to your imagination. Examples might be using them at your tailgate or other professional baseball related party. Players / Teams who answer questions incorrectly may have to perform a required action, or winners may receive special prizes. Let us know what other games you come up with!

Have fun!

1) When was the Twins' nickname officially adopted by the team?

Answers begin on page 17

    A)   1961
    B)   1962
    C)   1963
    D)   1964

2) What are the Twins' official colors?

    A)   Royal Blue, Red and White
    B)   Royal Blue and Red
    C)   Navy Blue and Red
    D)   Navy Blue, Red and White

3) What is the name of the Twins' current home stadium?

    A)   Hubert H. Humphrey Metrodome
    B)   Siebert Baseball Stadium
    C)   Target Field
    D)   Metropolitan Stadium

4) What year did the Twins join the American League?

    A)   1894
    B)   1901
    C)   1905
    D)   1908

5) What year did the Twins move to Minnesota?

    A) 1959
    B) 1960
    C) 1961
    D) 1962

6) In which American League Division do the Twins play?

    A) West
    B) Central
    C) North
    D) East

7) When was the most recent season the Twins won greater than 100 games?

    A) 1965
    B) 1970
    C) 2006
    D) 2010

8) Who has the longest tenure managing the Twins?

    A) Ron Gardenhire
    B) Tom Kelly
    C) Clark Griffith
    D) Bucky Harris

9) Which Twins' trio recorded two triple plays in a single game?

    A) Gaetti-Castino-Hrbek
    B) Gaetti-Teufel-Hrbek
    C) Gaetti-Lombardozzi-Hrbek
    D) Gaetti-Newman-Hrbek

10) Which of the following one-time baseball players was on the Twins' coaching staff?

    A) Tony Oliva
    B) Rick Stelmaszek
    C) Terry Crowley
    D) Ron Gardenhire

11) Who was the Twins' opponent in their most recent World Series appearance?

    A) St. Louis Cardinals
    B) Atlanta Braves
    C) Los Angeles Dodges
    D) San Francisco Giants

12) The Twins won the American League Pennant greater than 10 times.

    A) True
    B) False

13) Where did the Twins play in Washington, D.C. before moving to Minnesota?

 A) National Park
 B) Senator Park
 C) Griffith Stadium
 D) American League Park

14) Which Twin was nicknamed "Zorro"?

 A) Zoilo Versalles
 B) Tony Oliva
 C) Kirby Puckett
 D) Cesar Tovar

15) Minnesota's stadium has a seating capacity greater than 60,000.

 A) True
 B) False

16) Who is the Twins' current manager?

 A) Rick Anderson
 B) Joe Vavra
 C) Ron Gardenhire
 D) Steve Liddle

17) Who did the Twins play in the 2006 American League Division Series?

    A)   Toronto Blue Jays
    B)   New York Yankees
    C)   Baltimore Orioles
    D)   Oakland Athletics

18) What year did the Twins play in their first-ever World Series?

    A)   1923
    B)   1924
    C)   1925
    D)   1927

19) Who holds the Twins' career record for games pitched?

    A)   Walter Johnson
    B)   Eddie Guardado
    C)   Jim Kaat
    D)   Rick Aguilera

20) Who hit the most home runs for the Twins in 2010?

    A)   Delmon Young
    B)   Jason Kubel
    C)   Justin Morneau
    D)   Jim Thome

21) With which college football team did the Twins share the Hubert H. Humphrey Superdome?

    A) St. Paul College
    B) St. Cloud State University
    C) University of Minnesota
    D) Minnesota State University

22) What year did the Twins win their first-ever World Series?

    A) 1924
    B) 1925
    C) 1933
    D) 1965

23) How many total runs did the Twins score in the 2010 regular season?

    A) 775
    B) 778
    C) 781
    D) 784

24) Did the Twins win greater than 95 games in the 2010 regular season?

    A) Yes
    B) No

25) Who was the most recent Twin to win the title of American League Most Valuable Player?

    A) Joe Mauer
    B) Rod Carew
    C) Justin Morneau
    D) Harmon Killebrew

26) What nickname did the team go by immediately prior to becoming the Twins?

    A) Kansas City Blues
    B) Minnesota Twinkies
    C) Minnesota Golden Gophers
    D) Washington Senators

27) Who was the most recent Twin to win a Cy Young Award?

    A) Eddie Guardado
    B) Joe Nathan
    C) Johan Santana
    D) Frank Viola

28) Who is the only Twin to pitch greater than 5,000 innings in his career?

    A) Jim Kaat
    B) Bert Blyleven
    C) Camilo Pascual
    D) Walter Johnson

29) Glenn Borgmann had an unassisted triple play in 1976.

    A) True
    B) False

30) Which player has had his jersey number retired by the Twins and another team?

    A) Kirby Puckett
    B) Rod Carew
    C) Harmon Killebrew
    D) Kent Hrbek

31) Since 1961, how many times has a Twins' pitcher won 20 or greater games?

    A) 13
    B) 14
    C) 15
    D) 17

32) How many times have the Twins won 100 or greater games in a season?

    A) 1
    B) 2
    C) 3
    D) 4

33) Which of the choices below is not a radio show broadcasted on the Twins Radio Network?

   A) "Talkin' Twins"
   B) "The Ron Gardenhire Show"
   C) "Extra Innings Show"
   D) "Twins Will Win"

34) How many triple plays have been recorded in Twins' history?

   A) 20
   B) 24
   C) 31
   D) 35

35) Did the Twins have a winning record at the midseason break in 2010?

   A) Yes
   B) No

36) Which Twins' pitcher had the most wins in 2010?

   A) Scott Baker
   B) Francisco Liriano
   C) Kevin Slowey
   D) Carl Pavano

37) Which Twin holds the team's career records for at-bats, runs, hits, doubles and triples?

A) Sam Rice
B) Rod Carew
C) Harmon Killebrew
D) Kirby Puckett

38) Against which American League team did the Twins have the highest winning percentage during the 2010 regular season?

A) Los Angeles Angels of Anaheim
B) Cleveland Indians
C) Baltimore Orioles
D) Kansas City Royals

39) All time, how many World Series have the Twins won?

A) 2
B) 3
C) 4
D) 5

40) What year did the "M" insignia first appear on Twins' caps?

A) 1961
B) 1973
C) 1979
D) 1987

41) Which Twin had the most hits in the 2002 American League Division Series?

    A) Cristian Guzmán
    B) A.J. Pierzynski
    C) Torii Hunter
    D) Doug Mientkiewicz

42) Since 1961, how many times have the Twins scored greater than 800 runs in a season?

    A) 4
    B) 5
    C) 6
    D) 8

43) Which of the following Twins' pitchers threw greater than 10 shutouts in a season?

    A) Walter Johnson
    B) Bob Porterfield
    C) Camilo Pascual
    D) Bert Blyleven

44) How many Twins were selected to the 2010 All-Star team?

    A) 1
    B) 2
    C) 3
    D) 4

45) Since 1961, what is the Twins' record for most grand slams in a season?

    A) 5
    B) 6
    C) 7
    D) 8

46) Since 1961, what are the most Twins selected as All-Stars in a single season?

    A) 4
    B) 5
    C) 6
    D) 8

47) How many Twins' managers lasted one season or less?

    A) 5
    B) 7
    C) 8
    D) 10

48) How many hits did the Twins' pitching staff have in 2010?

    A) 1
    B) 2
    C) 3
    D) 5

49) What is the nickname of the AAA team affiliated with the Minnesota Twins?

    A)   Rochester Red Wings
    B)   Ft. Myers Miracle
    C)   New Britain Rock Cats
    D)   Beloit Snappers

50) When was the first-ever season the Minnesota Twins had a winning record against the Chicago White Sox?

    A)   1908
    B)   1910
    C)   1911
    D)   1913

Prior to the Twins moving to Minnesota, the Minneapolis Lakers headed for Los Angeles. Interest in the basketball team had diminished, due in part to the alienation suffered by fans from the neighboring city of St. Paul. Therefore, when the Twins relocated to the area, then-owner Calvin Griffith decided to make an attempt to appease both cities. He wanted to name the team the Twin Cities Twins, but Major League Baseball would not allow it. However, MLB did allow the team to use the "TC" insignia on their caps. In fact, it was used exclusively on their ball caps until 1987. That year, in addition to using a new alternate insignia on their caps, the team began using the "TC" logo on a jersey sleeve. Today one of the team's alternate caps bears the "M" insignia. Fans from St. Paul know that it stands for Minnesota, not Minneapolis. The "TC" remains the primary team logo to this day and St. Paul and Minneapolis fans are united by their support of the team.

1) A – 1961 (The team was named after Minnesota's Twin Cities.)
2) D – Navy Blue, Red and White
3) C – Target Field (It has been their home field since 2010.)
4) B – 1901 (The Twins were one of the American League's original eight teams.)
5) C – 1961 (They moved to Minnesota from Washington, D.C.)
6) B – Central (They joined the division in 1994.)
7) A – 1965 (The Twins recorded 102 wins and 60 losses.)
8) B – Tom Kelly (He served as manager from 1986-2001.)
9) D – Gaetti-Newman-Hrbek (The Twins are the only team to record two triple plays in a single game. This happened on July 17, 1990, at a game against the Boston Red Sox.)
10) A – Tony Oliva (He played for the Twins from 1962-76 and was on the coaching staff from 1976-78 and then again from 1985-91.)
11) B – Atlanta Braves (1991 World Series)

12) B – False (Minnesota has won six American League Pennants.)

13) C – Griffith Stadium (It was home to the Twins [then the Washington Senators] from 1911-60.)

14) A – Zoilo Versalles (Zorro can even be found on his 1961 baseball cards.)

15) B – False (Seating capacity of Target Field is only 39,504.)

16) C – Ron Gardenhire (He has been manager since 2002.)

17) D – Oakland Athletics (Minnesota lost the series, 0-3.)

18) B – 1924 (They played the New York Giants.)

19) A – Walter Johnson (802 games from 1907-27)

20) D – Jim Thome (25 home runs)

21) C – University of Minnesota (The Golden Gophers football team played there from 1982-2008. Their baseball team occasionally played in the Metrodome between 1985 and 2009.)

22) A – 1924 (Minnesota won the series, 4-3, against the New York Giants.)

23) C – 781 (Twenty-one different players scored runs in 2010.)

24) B – No (They won 94 games [94-68].)

25) A – Joe Mauer (He won the award in 2009.)

26) D – Washington Senators (They were known as the Nationals and Senators.)

27) C – Johan Santana (He won the Cy Young Award twice [2004 and 2006].)

28) D – Walter Johnson (5,914.2 innings from 1907-27)

29) B – False (Glenn Borgmann teamed up with Luis Gomez to record a triple play at the Chicago Cubs.)

30) B – Rod Carew (His number [#29] was also retired by the California Angels.)

31) C – 15 (Camilo Pascual and Jim Perry have had two 20-win seasons.)

32) A – 1 (This only happened in 1965, when they won 102 games.)

33) D – "Twins Will Win" (The Twins Radio Network has 162 affiliate stations broadcasting in five states.)

34) C – 31 (Twenty as the Washington Nationals and 11 as the Minnesota Twins)

35) A – Yes (The Twins were 46-42 at the All-Star break.)

36) D – Carl Pavano (17 wins)

37) A – Sam Rice (He amassed 8,934 at-bats, 1,466 runs, 2,889 hits, 479 doubles and 183 triples from 1915-34.)

38) D – Kansas City Royals (Minnesota also had a .722 winning percentage against the Chicago White Sox.)

39) B – 3 (1924, 1987 and 1991)

40) D – 1987 (The team kept the "TC" logo on their cap until that time.)

41) B – A.J. Pierzynski (He had seven hits, four RBIs, and one home run.)

42) C – 15 (Their most recent 800-plus run season was 2009 when they had 817.)

43) A – Walter Johnson (Johnson recorded 11 shutouts in 1913.)

44) B – 2 (Joe Mauer and Justin Morneau)

45) D – 8 (The team tallied eight gland slams In 1961.)

46) C – 6 (In 1965, Earl Battey, Mudcat Grant, Jimmie Hall, Harmon Killebrew, Tony Oliva and Zoilo Versalles were selected.)

47) B – 7 (Jim Manning, Malachi Kittridge, Patsy Donovan, George McBride, Clyde Milan, Donie Bush and Billy Martin)

48) C – 3 (All were hits by Jon Rauch.)

49) A – Rochester Red Wings (They have been the Twins' Triple-A affiliate since 2003.)

50) B – 1910 (They had a 13-9 record against the Chicago White Sox.)

Note: All answers valid as of the end of the 2010 season, unless otherwise indicated in the question itself.

1) What was Harmon Killebrew's nickname while playing for the Twins?

Answers begin on page 37

    A) "Hammerin' Harmon"
    B) "Homerin' Harmon"
    C) "Home Run Harmon"
    D) None of the above

2) What jersey number did Twins' great Kirby Puckett wear?

    A) #29
    B) #33
    C) #34
    D) #35

3) How many players have been inducted into the National Baseball Hall of Fame with the Twins as their primary team?

    A) 4
    B) 6
    C) 8
    D) 10

4) What were the total construction costs of Target Field?

    A) $392.0 million
    B) $522.6 million
    C) $544.4 million
    D) $565.3 million

5) Did the Twins have a winning record on the road during the regular season in 2010?

    A) Yes
    B) No

6) How many times did the Twins sweep a series during the 2010 regular season?

    A) 7
    B) 9
    C) 10
    D) 12

7) When was the first time a Twin hit 40 or greater home runs in a single season?

    A) 1954
    B) 1957
    C) 1959
    D) 1961

8) How many Twins have been named the American League Most Valuable Player?

    A) 5
    B) 6
    C) 7
    D) 8

9) Since 1901, the Twins have had more winning seasons in Minnesota than in Washington, D.C.

   A) True
   B) False

10) Which American League opponent have the Twins played the fewest times during the regular season?

   A) Toronto Blue Jays
   B) Seattle Mariners
   C) Tampa Bay Rays
   D) Texas Rangers

11) What is the Twins' winning percentage against the White Sox since 1961?

   A) .523
   B) .531
   C) .558
   D) .604

12) Since 1968, how many times has a Twin led the American League in saves?

   A) 2
   B) 3
   C) 4
   D) 5

13) How many times have Twins' pitchers been awarded the Cy Young Award?

A) 3
B) 4
C) 5
D) 6

14) When did the Twins record their first-ever winning season in the American League?

A) 1912
B) 1913
C) 1914
D) 1915

15) What is the Twins' record for the most hits as a team in a single season?

A) 1,614
B) 1,625
C) 1,633
D) 1,656

16) Has any Twin ever hit greater than four grand slams in a single season?

A) Yes
B) No

17) What is the Twins' record for fewest errors as a team during the regular season?

A) 69
B) 72
C) 74
D) 78

18) Which Twins' pitcher had the lowest ERA in 2010 (mini mum 50 innings pitched)?

A) Brian Duensing
B) Jesse Crain
C) Matt Guerrier
D) Jon Rauch

19) How many Twins have been walked 125 or greater times in a single season?

A) 8
B) 9
C) 10
D) 11

20) The Twins have won greater than 10,000 all-time regular-season games since joining the American League.

A) True
B) False

21) Which team have the Twins played the most (number of series played) in the World Series?

    A) Pittsburgh Pirates
    B) Los Angeles Dodgers
    C) San Francisco Giants
    D) St. Louis Cardinals

22) Since 1961, which Twins batter holds the club record for the most strikeouts in a nine-inning game?

    A) Bobby Darwin
    B) Sandy Valdespino
    C) Roy Smalley
    D) Bob Allison

23) How much is the contract Joe Mauer signed with the Twins in 2010?

    A) $178 million
    B) $182 million
    C) $184 million
    D) $192 million

24) Who was the Twins' most recent Gold Glove winner?

    A) Joe Mauer
    B) Torii Hunter
    C) Kirby Puckett
    D) Zoilo Versalles

25) Who was the Twins' manager in their first-ever season?

A) Malachi Kittridge
B) Tom Loftus
C) Patsy Donovan
D) Jim Manning

26) Who is the Twins' current pitching coach?

A) Dick Such
B) Eric Rasmussen
C) Rick Anderson
D) Rick Stelmaszek

27) Is the rivalry between the Twins and the White Sox the longest running rivalry in Major League Baseball?

A) Yes
B) No

28) Who is the only Twin to be named All-Star MVP?

A) Rod Carew
B) Kirby Puckett
C) Tony Oliva
D) Harmon Killebrew

29) How many seasons have the Twins finished the regular season in first place?

    A) 11
    B) 12
    C) 13
    D) 14

30) How many teams had a winning record against the Twins in the Twins' first-ever season?

    A) 1
    B) 2
    C) 3
    D) 4

31) Which award did the Twins' Michael Cuddyer receive following the 2009 season?

    A) Carl R. Pohlad Award
    B) Charles O. Johnson Award
    C) Calvin R. Griffith Award
    D) Mike Augustin Award

32) Since 1961, against which American League team do the Twins have their highest all-time winning percentage (minimum 500 games played)?

    A) Kansas City Royals
    B) Chicago White Sox
    C) Cleveland Indians
    D) Detroit Tigers

33) How many times have Twins' pitchers recorded 18 strikeouts in a single game?

A) 1
B) 2
C) 3
D) No Twins' pitcher has accomplished this

34) How many times have the Twins played the New York Yankees in the American League Division Series?

A) 3
B) 4
C) 5
D) 6

35) Since 1961, what is the Twins' record for the most runs allowed in a single game?

A) 20
B) 21
C) 22
D) 23

36) Johan Santana is the most recent Twin to wear jersey #57.

A) True
B) False

37) Who was Minnesota's first-ever opponent in Target Field?

    A) Cleveland Indians
    B) Boston Red Sox
    C) New York Yankees
    D) Chicago White Sox

38) Since 1961, how many times has a Twin hit for the cycle (single, double, triple and home run in the same game)?

    A) 8
    B) 9
    C) 10
    D) 11

39) Which Twins pitcher holds the team record for the lowest ERA in a season?

    A) Eddie Guardado
    B) Matt Guerrier
    C) Walter Johnson
    D) Joe Nathan

40) Has any Twin had a batting average of .400 or greater for a single season (minimum 50 at-bats)?

    A) Yes
    B) No

41) Who holds the Twins' career record for stolen bases?

    A) George Case
    B) Sam Rice
    C) Rod Carew
    D) Clyde Milan

42) How many players have played greater than 2,000 games as a Twin?

    A) 3
    B) 4
    C) 5
    D) 6

43) What is the nickname of the AA team affiliated with the Minnesota Twins?

    A) GCL Twins
    B) Fort Myers Miracle
    C) New Britain Rock Cats
    D) Beloit Snappers

44) How many times have the Twins been swept in the World Series?

    A) 0
    B) 1
    C) 2
    D) 3

45) How many Twins had their jersey number retired, but are not members of the National Baseball Hall of Fame?

   A) 1
   B) 2
   C) 3
   D) 4

46) When did the Twins last host the All-Star Game?

   A) 1983
   B) 1984
   C) 1985
   D) 1986

47) How many players have had their jersey number retired by the Twins?

   A) 4
   B) 5
   C) 6
   D) 7

48) How many times did Tom Kelly win American League Manager of the Year as a Twin?

   A) 2
   B) 3
   C) 4
   D) 5

49) In which decade did the Twins have the highest regular-season winning percentage?

    A) 1920s
    B) 1930s
    C) 1960s
    D) 2000s

50) How many Twins have won the World Series Most Valuable Player Award?

    A) 1
    B) 2
    C) 3
    D) 4

The history of the nicknames of the Minnesota Twins' franchise is a veritable name game that has crossed the continent. The franchise first began in Washington, D.C. as the Washington Nationals. Even though their official name was the Nationals, fans called them the Senators. Prior to the American League team, Washington D.C. was home to the National League Washington Senators. To avoid confusion, the new AL franchise chose the name of Nationals. Despite the team's efforts however, fans not only referred to the team as the Senators, they also nicknamed the team the "Nats." At the time, no one knew for sure whether this nickname came from Se*nat*ors or *Nat*ionals. After half a century, the team finally changed the official name to the Senators. In 1959, the name of Senators appeared on the team's jerseys for the first time. The name stayed until the team relocated to Minnesota. After relocating, Washington D.C. was granted yet another expansion team which was, once again, named the Senators. Eventually, that team moved to Texas, where they became the Rangers in 1972. Today's Washington Nationals are yesterday's Montreal Expos. And the name game goes on.

1) A – "Hammerin' Harmon" (He was also known as "Killer.")

2) C – #34 (Puckett wore this number from 1984-95.)

3) A – 4 (Rod Carew, Harmon Killebrew, Kirby Puckett and, most recently, Bert Blyleven have been inducted. Additionally, four players were inducted as Washington Senators.)

4) C – $544.4 million (These costs include site acquisition and infrastructure. Construction took over two years.)

5) A – Yes (The Twins had a 41-40 road-game record.)

6) B – 9 (Detroit, Texas [2], Kansas City [2], Seattle, Oakland, Chicago White Sox and Cleveland)

7) B – 1957 (Roy Sievers hit 42 home runs, leading the league that season.)

8) A – 5 (Zoilo Versalles [1965], Harmon Killebrew [1969], Rod Carew [1977], Justin Morneau [2006] and Joe Mauer [2009])

9) A – True (The Twins have 24 winning seasons in Minnesota and 18 winning seasons in Washington, D.C.)

10) C – Tampa Bay Rays (They have played 100 times in the regular season.)

11) B – .531 (407-358-3)

12) D – 5 (Al Worthington [17 saves in 1968], Ron Perranoski [31 in 1969 and 34 in 1970], Mike Marshall [32 in 1979] and Eddie Guardado [45 in 2002])

13) B – 4 (Jim Perry [1970], Frank Viola [1988] and Johan Santana [2004 and 2006])

14) A – 1912 (Playing as the Washington Senators, they recorded a 91-61 record, placing second in the American League.)

15) C– 1,633 (This team record was set in 1996.)

16) B – No (Bob Allison [1962], Rod Carew [1976], Kent Hrbek [1985], Kirby Puckett [1992] and Torii Hunter [2007] all hit three grand slams in a season.)

17) C – 74 (The Twins set this club record in 2002.)

18) A – Brian Duensing (Duensing had an ERA of 2.62 in 130.2 innings pitched in 2010.)

19) A – 8 (Eddie Yost tops the list, by being walked 151 times in 1956.)

20) B – False (The Twins have won 8,326 games.)

21) C – San Francisco Giants (They [then-New York Giants] played in the 1924 and 1933 World Series.)

22) D – Bob Allison (He was struck out five times against the Detroit Tigers on Sept. 2, 1965. This ties him for the MLB record.)

23) C – $184 million (Mauer signed an eight-year contract extension for 2011-18, earning $23 million each season.)

24) A – Joe Mauer (He was awarded the Gold Glove for AL catchers in 2010.)

25) D – Jim Manning (Manning lasted only one season [1901].)

26) C – Rick Anderson (The Twins hired him as primary pitching coach in 2002.)

27) B – No (The Twins-White Sox rivalry first surfaced in the 2000s. The Yankees-Red Sox rivalry has been going strong for over 100 years.)

28) B – Kirby Puckett (In 1993, he was named All-Star MVP.)

29) D – 14 (Four times they finished first in the American League, four times in the AL West and six times in the AL Central.)

30) A – 1 (The Detroit Tigers had an 11-9 record against the Twins [then-Washington Senators] in 1901.)

31) B – Charles O. Johnson Award (It is awarded to the Most Improved Twin. He was also awarded the Bob Allison Leadership Award in 2009 and 2010.)

32) D – Detroit Tigers (The Twins have a .538 winning percentage against the Tigers [378-325-1].)

33) D – No Twins' pitcher has accomplished this (Johan Santana leads the team with 17 strikeouts in eight innings versus the Texas Rangers in 2007.)

34) B – 4 (2003, 2004, 2009 and 2010)

35) D – 23 (The Kansas City Royals defeated the Twins, 23-6, on April 6, 1974.)

36) A – True (Santana wore #57 from 2000-07.)

37) B – Boston Red Sox (On April 12, 2010, Minnesota defeated the Red Sox, 5-2.)

38) C – 10 (Jason Kubel and Michael Cuddyer both hit for the cycle in the 2009 season.)

39) C – Walter Johnson (He recorded a 1.14 ERA [371.2 innings pitched] in 1913.)

40) B – No (Rod Carew had a .388 batting average in 1977 [616 at-bats].)

41) D – Clyde Milan (Milan had 495 stolen bases from 1907-22.)

42) A – 3 (Harmon Killebrew [2,329], Sam Rice [2,307] and Joe Judge [2,084])

43) C – New Britain Rock Cats (The New Britain Rock Cats have been the Twins' AA affiliate since 1995.)

44) A – 0 (They have won at least one game in each World Series played.)

45) B – 2 (Tony Oliva and Kent Hrbek)

46) C – 1985 (They also hosted the 1965 All-Star Game, held at Metropolitan Stadium.)

47) B – 5 (Twins' retired numbers include Harmon Killebrew's #3, Tony Oliva's #6, Kent Hrbek's #14, Rod Carew's #29 and Kirby Puckett's #34. League wide in 1997, #42 was retired in honor of Jackie Robinson.)

48) A – 2 (He won UPI American League Manager of the year in 1987 and 1991. He was also awarded the TSN AL Manager of the Year and the AL Manager of the Year in 1991.)

49) C – 1960s (They had a .536 winning percentage [862-747-5].)

50) B – 2 (Frank Viola [1987] and Jack Morris [1991] won the World Series Most Valuable Player as starting pitchers.)

Note: All answers valid as of the end of the 2010 season, unless otherwise indicated in the question itself.

1) Since 1961, who holds the Twins' record for the most career grand slams?

Answers begin on page 56

    A) Harmon Killebrew
    B) Kent Hrbek
    C) Jason Kubel
    D) Torii Hunter

2) How did the Twins' Bert Blyleven earn the nickname of the "Frying Dutchman?"

    A) His pitching ability
    B) He was born in the Netherlands
    C) He set his teammates' shoelaces on fire
    D) He loved fried foods

3) When was the most recent season the Twins failed to go .500?

    A) 1999
    B) 2000
    C) 2005
    D) 2007

4) Which Twins' manager has the most career wins?

    A) Bucky Harris
    B) Clark Griffith
    C) Ron Gardenhire
    D) Tom Kelly

5) Dean Chance is the only Twin to throw greater than one no-hitter.

    A) True
    B) False

6) Which of the following positions is not represented by a Twin in the National Baseball Hall of Fame?

    A)   First Baseman
    B) Center Fielder
    C) Catcher
    D) Right Fielder

7) Which Twins' pitcher has the highest career winning percentage [minimum 75 career wins]?

    A) Walter Johnson
    B) Firpo Marberry
    C) Jim Perry
    D) Johan Santana

8) How many pitchers did the Twins use during the 2010 regular season?

    A) 19
    B) 20
    C) 21
    D) 22

9) Since 1961, what is the Twins' winning percentage against the Cleveland Indians?

    A) .529
    B) .530
    C) .531
    D) .532

10) Tom Kelly is the only manager to have his jersey number retired by the Twins.

    A) True
    B) False

11) Which of the following Twins' career records is not held by Harmon Killebrew?

    A) Walks
    B) Strikeouts
    C) Runs Batted In
    D) Batting Average

12) Which Twins' manager has the highest career winning percentage in postseason play?

    A) Sam Mele
    B) Ron Gardenhire
    C) Tom Kelly
    D) Bucky Harris

13) What are the most team errors the Twins have committed in a single season?

A) 311
B) 316
C) 320
D) 323

14) Which Twins' pitcher did not win a Gold Glove?

A) Tony Oliva
B) Bert Blyleven
C) Chuck Knoblauch
D) Gary Gaetti

15) Which Twins' manager had the highest winning percentage (minimum three seasons)?

A) Walter Johnson
B) Ron Gardenhire
C) Bucky Harris
D) Sam Mele

16) How many Twins have recorded over 250 stolen bases?

A) 4
B) 5
C) 6
D) 7

17) Who was the most recent Twin to be named the American League Home Run Champion?

   A) Gary Gaetti
   B) Justin Morneau
   C) Harmon Killebrew
   D) Torii Hunter

18) Did any Twins' pitcher hit a home run in 2010?

   A) Yes
   B) No

19) When was the most recent season the leading player for the Twins had fewer than 75 RBIs?

   A) 1968
   B) 1980
   C) 1998
   D) 1999

20) What is the current marked distance to the center field wall at Target Field?

   A) 399'
   B) 403'
   C) 404'
   D) 411'

21) Who was the most recent Twins' pitcher to lead the team in strikeouts, wins and ERA in the same season?

    A) Rick Reed
    B) Scott Baker
    C) Johan Santana
    D) Joe Mays

22) Who is the Twins' current team captain?

    A) Michael Cuddyer
    B) Joe Mauer
    C) Jason Kubel
    D) No official team captain

23) Tony Oliva was the first player to wear jersey #37 for the Twins in Minnesota.

    A) True
    B) False

24) When was the most recent season the Twins, as a team, had a batting average of .275 or greater?

    A) 2003
    B) 2006
    C) 2008
    D) 2010

25) Did Harmon Killebrew end his career with the Twins?

    A) Yes
    B) No

26) Who was the only Twin to play in every game during the 2010 regular season?

    A) Denard Span
    B) Michael Cuddyer
    C) Delmon Young
    D) None of the above

27) Who hit the most home runs for the Twins in the 2010 postseason?

    A) Joe Mauer
    B) Orlando Hudson
    C) Jason Kubel
    D) Denard Span

28) Who did the Twins play in their home opener in 2010?

    A) Los Angeles Angels of Anaheim
    B) Chicago White Sox
    C) Boston Red Sox
    D) Kansas City Royals

29) Has any Twins' pitcher ever recorded 150 or greater career saves?

    A) Yes
    B) No

30) What is the combined winning percentage of Twins' managers who lasted one season or less?

    A) .440
    B) .463
    C) .486
    D) .501

31) Which other sports teams shared Metropolitan Stadium with the Minnesota Twins?

    A) Minnesota Kicks
    B) Minnesota Vikings
    C) Minneapolis Millers
    D) All of the Above

32) What are the most consecutive losses the Twins have ever had in one season?

    A) 14
    B) 16
    C) 18
    D) 19

33) Against which team did the Twins hit four consecutive home runs on May 2, 1964?

    A) Milwaukee Brewers
    B) Kansas City Royals
    C) Cleveland Indians
    D) Chicago White Sox

34) Since 1961, what are the fewest losses by the Twins in one season?

    A) 60
    B) 62
    C) 63
    D) 66

35) Did any Twin have greater than 250 assists in the 2010 regular season?

    A) Yes
    B) No

36) Which player holds the Twins' record for most at-bats in a single season?

    A) Sam Rice
    B) Tony Oliva
    C) Harmon Killebrew
    D) Kirby Puckett

37) Who was Minnesota's first round draft pick in 2010?

A) Niko Goodrum
B) Alex Wimmers
C) Kyle Gibson
D) Matthew Bashore

38) Who holds the Twins' record for runs scored in a career?

A) Sam Rice
B) Chuck Knoblauch
C) Joe Judge
D) Rod Carew

39) What are the most pure steals of home base by a Twin in a single season?

A) 2
B) 3
C) 4
D) 5

40) When was the most recent season the leading hitter for the Twins had a batting average below .300?

A) 2002
B) 2004
C) 2005
D) 2007

41) Who is the only Twins' pitcher to win the American League Triple Crown more than once?

 A) Johan Santana
 B) Walter Johnson
 C) Brad Radke
 D) Jim Kaat

42) What is the Twins' record for the most innings played in a single game?

 A) 19
 B) 20
 C) 21
 D) 22

43) Has Johan Santana ever won a Gold Glove?

 A) Yes
 B) No

44) Who was the most recent Twin to hit an inside-the-park home run?

 A) Justin Morneau
 B) Jason Kubel
 C) Joe Mauer
 D) Michael Cuddyer

45) How many Twins have a career on-base percentage of .400 or greater?

A) 1
B) 2
C) 3
D) 4

46) What color are the Twins' current away uniforms?

A) Gray with Pinstripes
B) White with Pinstripes
C) Solid Gray
D) Solid Navy Blue

47) How many home runs did the Twins score in 2010 night games?

A) 87
B) 89
C) 91
D) 94

48) How many Twins have won the Roberto Clemente Award?

A) 2
B) 3
C) 4
D) 5

49) Denard Span had a better batting average against right-handed pitchers than left-handed pitchers in 2010.

   A) True
   B) False

50) How many times was Chuck Knoblauch hit by pitch in his career as a Twin?

   A) 71
   B) 73
   C) 74
   D) 76

Metropolitan Stadium, home of the Minnesota Twins from 1961-81, was built in 1956. It was originally built for the Minnesota Millers, a minor league baseball team at the time. The stadium had short foul lines, 343 feet to left and 330 to right. This made it a hitter's dream park and may have led to some of Harmon Killebrew's stellar home run statistics. Although this may have been an advantage for the Twins, the stadium shortly began to show its age. By the 1970s, for example, there were broken railings on the third level. After the AFL-NFL merger, the Minnesota Vikings demanded a new stadium, one that could seat at least 50,000 spectators. The Twins decided that the time was right for a move of their own, and they, too, relocated to the new stadium. Metropolitan Stadium sat empty for a few years, until finally being demolished in 1985. Opened in 1992, the Mall of America now stands in the footprint of the old stadium. But this landmark honors the location's storied past, with a brass plaque representing home plate in the floor of the mall. There is also a red stadium chair, mounted high on the wall, showing where Harmon Killebrew hit his 520-foot, upper-deck home run back in 1967. It was his longest home run and the longest-ever at Metropolitan Stadium.

1) A – Harmon Killebrew (Killebrew had 10 grand slams from 1961-74.)

2) C – His favorite practical joke was to set his teammates' shoelaces on fire.

3) D – 2007 (The Twins recorded a .488 winning percentage [79-83].)

4) D – Tom Kelly (He had 1140 wins during his tenure [1986-2001].)

5) B – False (Chance pitched two no-hitters [1967]. Walter Johnson also pitched two [1920 and 1924].)

6) C – Catcher (The only positions represented are pitcher, left fielder, right fielder, center fielder and first baseman.)

7) D – Johan Santana (He had a .716 winning percentage [78-31] from 2000-06.)

8) B – 20 (Innings pitched ranged from 1.0 inning to 221 innings.)

9) A – .529 (The Twins have a 406-361-3 all-time record against the Indians.)

10) B – False (No Twins' manager has had their jersey number retired.)

11) D – Batting Average (Killebrew does not show up in the top ten.)

12) C – Tom Kelly (He has a .667 winning percentage in postseason games [16-8].)

13) D – 323 (This team record was set in 1901.)

14) B – Bert Blyleven (He has an impressive resume, including two All-Star selections, a no-hitter and recent induction into the National Baseball Hall of Fame, but he was never awarded a Gold Glove.)

15) A – Walter Johnson (He has a .570 winning percentage [350-264].)

16) B – 5 (Clyde Milan [495], Sam Rice [346], George Case [321], Chuck Knoblauch [276] and Rod Carew [271])

17) C – Harmon Killebrew (He was named AL Home Run Champion six times [1959, 1962-64, 1967 and 1969].)

18) B – No (The pitching staff only had three hits in 2010.)

19) D – 1999 (Marty Cordova led the team with 70 RBIs.)

20) C – 404' (Distances range from 403' to 411' in center field.)

21) C – Johan Santana (In 2007, he won 15 games, pitched 235 strikeouts and recorded a 3.33 ERA.)

22) D – No official team captain (Some might consider Joe Mauer an unofficial team captain, but the Twins do not currently have an official team captain.)

23) A – True (Oliva wore #37 from 1962-64.)

24) C – 2008 (The team had a .279 batting average.)

25) B – No (He spent the 1975 season with the Kansas City Royals.)

26) D – None of the above (Michael Cuddyer led the team, playing in 157 games.)

27) B – Orlando Hudson (He scored one home run in the postseason. Michael Cuddyer also scored one.)

28) C – Boston Red Sox (The Twins won their home opener, 5-2.)

29) A – Yes (Rick Aguilera [254] and Joe Nathan [246])

30) B – .463 (This represents a 420-487 overall record for managers lasting one season or less.)

31) D – All of the Above (Minneapolis Millers [1956-60], Minnesota Vikings [1961-81] and Minnesota Kicks [1976-81])

32) C – 18 (The Washington Senators lost 18 straight games in both the 1948 and 1959 seasons.)

33) B – Kansas City Royals (Tony Oliva, Bob Allison, Jimmie Hall and Harmon Killebrew hit the home runs in the 11th inning.)

34) A – 60 (In 1965, the Twins went 102-60. They also had only 60 losses in the strike-shortened season of 1994.)

35) A – Yes (Orlando Hudson [374] and J.J. Hardy [289])

36) D – Kirby Puckett (He had 691 at-bats to lead the American League in 1985.)

37) B – Alex Wimmers (He was the #21 pick of the first round. Wimmers is a right-handed pitcher from Ohio State.)

38) A – Sam Rice (He scored 1,466 runs from 1915-33.)

39) B – 3 (Rod Carew stole home three times in 1969.)

40) D – 2007 (Joe Mauer led the team with a .293 batting average.)

41) B – Walter Johnson (He won the American League Triple Crown three times [1913, 1918 and 1924].)

42) D – 22 (On May 12, 1972, the Twins lost to the Milwaukee Brewers, 4-3, in a game lasting 5 hours, 47 minutes. This happened a second time when the Twins beat the Cleveland Indians, 5-4, in a six-hour, 17 minute game on Aug. 31, 1993.)

43) A – Yes (Santana won a Gold Glove in 2007 as pitcher.)

44) C – Joe Mauer (On July 21, 2007, he hit a three-run inside-the-park home run versus the Los Angeles Angels of Anaheim in the eighth inning.)

45) B – 2 (Ed Delahanty [.4112] and Joe Mauer [.4073])

46) C – Solid Gray (The away uniforms were changed for the 2010 season from navy pinstripes.)

47) D – 94 (Delmon Young led the team with 14 night-game home runs.)

48) B – 3 (Rod Carew [1977], Dave Winfield [1994] and Kirby Puckett [1996])

49) B – False (Span had a .256 batting average against right-handed pitchers and .279 against left-handed pitchers.)

50) C – 74 (He was hit by pitch 19 times during the 1996 season.)

Note: All answers valid as of the end of the 2010 season, unless otherwise indicated in the question itself.

1) Which Twins' manager is the only one enshrined in the National Baseball Hall of Fame as a manager?

Answers begin on page 75

   A) Walter Johnson
   B) Tom Kelly
   C) Clark Griffith
   D) Bucky Harris

2) Who was the first black player to play for the Twins?

   A) Carlos Paula
   B) Minnie Minoso
   C) Tom Alston
   D) Jay Heard

3) The Twins cancelled spring training from 1943-45 due to war time travel restrictions.

   A) True
   B) False

4) Where is the Twins' Latin American Baseball Academy located?

   A) San Juan, Puerto Rico
   B) Santo Domingo, Dominican Republic
   C) Boca Chica, Dominican Republic
   D) Ponce, Puerto Rico

5) The Twins were the first-ever team in MLB to play a black pitcher.

    A) True
    B) False

6) For what team did former Twin Bert Blyleven not play between 1976 and 1985?

    A) Cleveland Indians
    B) Texas Rangers
    C) California Angels
    D) Pittsburgh Pirates

7) What is the Twins' record for the most consecutive winning seasons?

    A) 5
    B) 6
    C) 7
    D) 8

8) Since 1961, how many teams has Minnesota played greater than 500 times in the regular season?

    A) 6
    B) 7
    C) 8
    D) 9

9) What feat did the Twins' Cesar Tovar accomplish on Sept. 22, 1968?

    A) Hit home run from each side of plate
    B) Hit for the cycle
    C) Played all nine positions
    D) None of the above

10) Which Twin has won the most Gold Gloves?

    A) Jim Kaat
    B) Kirby Puckett
    C) Torii Hunter
    D) Gary Gaetti

11) Which team did Bucky Harris not manage between his positions with the Twins?

    A) New York Yankees
    B) Boston Red Sox
    C) Detroit Tigers
    D) Chicago Cubs

12) Has any Twin led the American League in runs scored in a single season?

    A) Yes
    B) No

13) Which Twin was nicknamed the "Barney"?

    A) Bert Blyleven
    B) Beany Jacobson
    C) Goose Goslin
    D) Walter Johnson

14) Which Twin was the youngest member to be inducted into the National Baseball Hall of Fame?

    A) Kirby Puckett
    B) Rod Carew
    C) Walter Johnson
    D) Harmon Killebrew

15) What is the name of the series between the Twins and the White Sox?

    A) Border Battle
    B) Caddy Corner Battle
    C) I-94 Series
    D) The series is unnamed

16) Which Twin had the first-ever hit at Target Field?

    A) Denard Span
    B) Orlando Hudson
    C) Justin Morneau
    D) Joe Mauer

17) How many Twins batters' won the American League Triple Crown?

    A) 1
    B) 2
    C) 3
    D) No Twins' batter has won

18) When was the most recent season the Twins failed to hit greater than 100 team home runs?

    A) 1990
    B) 1992
    C) 1994
    D) 1999

19) Where do the Twins hold spring training?

    A) Naples, Fla.
    B) Port Charlotte, Fla.
    C) Ft. Myers, Fla.
    D) Sarasota, Fla.

20) Since 1961, who is the only Twins' pitcher to lead the team in strikeouts for six consecutive years?

    A) Camilo Pascual
    B) Bert Blyleven
    C) Frank Viola
    D) Johan Santana

21) All time, how many managers have the Twins had?

A) 27
B) 28
C) 29
D) 30

22) Who threw out the ceremonial first pitch for the first-ever game at Target Field?

A) Jerry Bell
B) Mike Opat
C) Dave Mansell
D) All of the Above

23) Which Twins' manager had the second highest career winning percentage (minimum three seasons)?

A) Bill Rigney
B) Ron Gardenhire
C) Sam Mele
D) Bucky Harris

24) Did the Twins win every game in 2010 when scoring five or more runs?

A) Yes
B) No

25) What is the Twins' record for the most times a player has been hit by pitch in a season?

   A) 62
   B) 63
   C) 65
   D) 67

26) Who hit the first home run for the Twins in their first-ever home game in Minnesota?

   A) Lenny Green
   B) Bob Allison
   C) Reno Bertoia
   D) Don Mincher

27) Since 1961, what year did the Twins have the highest home winning percentage?

   A) 1969
   B) 1977
   C) 1987
   D) 2002

28) Which of the following players did not win Minor League Player or Pitcher of the Year?

   A) Joe Mauer
   B) Chris Parmelee
   C) Francisco Liriano
   D) Matt Garza

29) Which decade did the Twins have the lowest winning percentage?

    A) 1900s
    B) 1940s
    C) 1950s
    D) 1990s

30) When was the most recent season the Twins had total home attendance of fewer than 2 million?

    A) 2002
    B) 2003
    C) 2004
    D) 2005

31) How many times have the Twins finished in first place in the American League and failed to win the World Series?

    A) 9
    B) 10
    C) 11
    D) 12

32) What is the lowest team batting average the Twins ever had in a single season?

    A) .218
    B) .223
    C) .229
    D) .237

33) Which pitcher holds the Twins' career record for most strikeouts?

A) Camilo Pascual
B) Bert Blyleven
C) Walter Johnson
D) Jim Kaat

34) Which Twins' pitcher won the American League Relief Man of the Year Award on two occasions?

A) Jeff Reardon
B) Joe Nathan
C) Bill Campbell
D) None of the above

35) Who was the most recent Twin to win American League Rookie of the Year?

A) Marty Cordova
B) Joe Mauer
C) Chuck Knoblauch
D) Denard Span

36) How many times has Minnesota lost in the American League Division Series?

A) 3
B) 4
C) 5
D) 6

37) How many times have the Twins shut out the opposing team in the World Series?

    A) 2
    B) 3
    C) 4
    D) 5

38) What was the lowest regular-season winning percentage of a Twins World Series Championship team?

    A) .525
    B) .552
    C) .586
    D) .597

39) What was the greatest number of pitchers used by the Twins in a single game of the 2002 ALCS?

    A) 4
    B) 5
    C) 6
    D) 7

40) Joe Mauer is the only Twin to ever score two home runs in a single inning.

    A) Yes
    B) No

41) What is the nickname of the Twins' Advanced A affiliate located in Ft. Myers, Fla.?

   A) Manatees
   B) Stone Crabs
   C) Threshers
   D) Miracle

42) Who was the most recent Twin to lead the American League in batting average?

   A) Kirby Puckett
   B) Joe Mauer
   C) Rod Carew
   D) Paul Molitor

43) What is the biggest-ever blown lead by the Twins?

   A) 10 runs
   B) 11 runs
   C) 12 runs
   D) 13 runs

44) What was the highest winning percentage of a Twins manager who lasted one season or less?

   A) .563
   B) .574
   C) .582
   D) .598

45) When was the most recent season the Twins failed to score 500 runs?

    A) 1968
    B) 1972
    C) 1981
    D) 1994

46) Who was the most recent Twin to lead the American League in RBIs?

    A) Kirby Puckett
    B) Justin Morneau
    C) Torii Hunter
    D) Paul Molitor

47) How many total no-hitters have been thrown by Twins' pitchers (includes perfect games)?

    A) 3
    B) 4
    C) 5
    D) 6

48) How many times have the Twins won 95 or greater games in a season without winning the World Series?

    A) 4
    B) 5
    C) 6
    D) 7

49) When was the first season Kirby Puckett played in the MLB All-Star Game?

    A) 1985
    B) 1986
    C) 1987
    D) 1988

50) Joe Mauer was the first Twin to receive a Gold Glove and American League MVP in the same year.

    A) True
    B) False

Without Target Field, the Minnesota Twins might not be the *Minnesota* Twins. Financial reasons, including the lack of revenue from suite leasing, a restrictive concession sales sharing agreement, and limited season-ticket quality seats in the Metrodome, led the Twins to push for their own baseball-only venue. It seemed as if the writing was on the wall when in 2002 MLB tagged the Twins for elimination due to their lack of financial sustainability. While a court decision required the Twins to play out their lease in the Metrodome, the team never gave up the dream of their own stadium. The Twins could have been moved to Portland, Las Vegas, Raleigh-Durham or even New Jersey, yet Minnesota was determined to hold on to their baseball team. Eventually the public and private sector approved a financial package to build a replacement stadium. On Jan. 4, 2010, in plenty of time for the upcoming season, the Minnesota Twins were at last handed the keys to their new home—Target Field.

1) D – Bucky Harris (He was inducted in 1975.)

2) A – Carlos Paula (His first game with the Senators was Sept. 6, 1954.)

3) B – False (While known as the Washington Senators, they held spring training in College Park, Md. to conserve rail transport during the war.)

4) C – Boca Chica, Dominican Republic (Their training complex is part of the Complejo Latinamericano de Beisbol, S.A., which also houses Arizona, the Chicago Cubs and Cincinnati.)

5) B – False (Dan Bankhead of the Brooklyn Dodgers was the first black pitcher in 1947.)

6) C – California Angels (Between his stints with the Twins, he played for the Rangers, Pirates, and Indians. After his second stint, he played for the Angels.)

7) B – 6 (The Twins enjoyed consecutive winning seasons from 2001-06.)

8) D – 9 (The Twins have played the Chicago White Sox and Cleveland Indians the most [770].)

9) C – Played all nine positions (He became the second player in Major League history to do this. Tovar was the first position player to start as pitcher.)

10) A – Jim Kaat (He won 11 straight Gold Glove awards as a Twin [1962-71].)

11) D – Chicago Cubs (Harris also managed the Philadelphia Phillies.)

12) A – Yes (George Case [102 runs in 1943], Bob Allison [99 in 1963], Tony Oliva [109 in 1964], Zoilo Versalles [126 in 1965] and Rod Carew [128 in 1977])

13) D – Walter Johnson (He got out of a speeding ticket when a teammate in the car told the police officer that he was Barney Oldfield, a race-car driver.)

14) A – Kirby Puckett (He was elected to the National Baseball Hall of Fame at age 41.)

15) D – The series is unnamed (The Twins-White Sox rivalry has yet to earn an unofficial nickname.)

16) B – Orlando Hudson (He singled to left field in the first inning.)

17) D – No Twins' batter has won (Killebrew led the league in home runs and RBIs in 1962 and 1969, but did not lead the league in batting average.)

18) A – 1990 (The Twins hit exactly 100 home runs.)

19) C – Ft. Myers, Fla. (Spring training has been held here since 1991. They play their games in Hammond Stadium.)

20) D – Johan Santana (He led the team in strikeouts from 2002-07.)

21) C – 29 (They started with Jim Manning in 1901. Ron Gardenhire is the current manager.)

22) D – All of the above (Jerry Bell, president of Twins Sports, Inc.; Mike Opat, Hennepin County Commissioner; and Dave Mansell, Mortenson Construction superintendent, all threw ceremonial first pitches at Target Field.)

23) D – Bucky Harris (From 1924-28, Harris had a .562 winning percentage [429-334].)

24) B – No (The Twins lost 11 games in 2010 in which they scored five or greater runs.)

25) C – 65 (In 1996, Twins were hit by pitch 65 times.)

26) D – Don Mincher (He hit a home run in the fourth inning against the Washington Senators on April 21, 1961.)

27) A – 1969 (They recorded a .704 winning percentage [57-23].)

28) B – Chris Parmelee (Mauer won Baseball America's award in 2003. Liriano and Garza won USA Today's award in 2005 and 2006, respectively.)

29) A – 1900s (They had a .366 winning percentage [480-833] for the decade.)

30) C – 2004 (The Twins had a home attendance of just 1,911,418.)

31) C – 11 (It has happened six times in the last decade [2002-04, 2006, 2009 and 2010]. Other years include 1925, 1933, 1965, 1969 and 1970.)

32) B – .223 (The team set this record in 1909.)

33) C – Walter Johnson (3,509 strikeouts from 1907-27)

34) D – None of the above (Bill Campbell [1976] and Joe Nathan [2009] each won the award once.)

35) A – Marty Cordova (In 1995, Cordova hit 24 home runs, had 84 RBIs and recorded a .277 batting average.)

36) C – 5 (2003, 2004, 2006, 2009 and 2010)

37) B – 3 (Game Four in 1925 [4-0], Game Three in 1933 [4-0], and Game Seven in 1991 [1-0])

38) A – .525 (The 1987 World Series Championship team had an 85-77 regular-season record.)

39) C – 6 (In Game Four [Radke, Santana, Hawkins, Romero, Jackson and Wells] and Game Five [Mays, Santana, Hawkins, Romero, Wells and Lohse])

40) B – No (Michael Cuddyer is the only Twin to score two home runs in a single inning. He did so in the seventh inning at Kansas City Royals on Aug. 23, 2009.)

41) D – Miracle (They have been a Twins' affiliate since 1992.)

42) B – Joe Mauer (He led the AL in 2006, 2008 and 2009.)

43) A – 10 runs (The Twins were leading the Cleveland Indians, 10-0, on Sept. 28, 1984, but ended up losing 10-11. They also were leading the Oakland Athletics, 12-2, on July 20, 2009, and lost 13-14.)

44) D – .598 (As manager in 1969, Billy Martin recorded a .598 winning percentage [97-65].)

45) C – 1981 (The Twins scored 378 runs during the strike-shortened season.)

46) A – Kirby Puckett (He led the American League in 1994 with 112 RBIs.)

47) D – 6 (Walter Johnson [July 1, 1920 at Boston Red Sox], Bobby Burke [Aug. 8, 1931 versus Boston Red Sox], Jack Kralick [Aug. 26, 1962 versus Kansas City Athletics], Dean Chance [Aug. 25, 1967 at Cleveland Indians], Scott Erickson [April 27, 1994 versus Milwaukee Brewers] and Eric Milton [Sept. 11, 1999 versus Anaheim Angels])

48) C – 6 (1925, 1933, 1965, 1969, 1970 and 2006)

49) B – 1986 (Puckett started his first All-Star game, in addition to starting five others.)

50) B – False (Zoilo Versalles was the first to win both awards in 1965. Mauer won both in 2009.)

Note: All answers valid as of the end of the 2010 season, unless otherwise indicated in the question itself.

1) How many Twins' managers have won at least one World Series?

Answers begin on page 83

A) 1
B) 2
C) 3
D) 4

2) All time, how many World Series games have the Twins lost by a single run?

A) 5
B) 6
C) 7
D) 8

3) How many overall No. 1 draft picks have the Twins had?

A) 1
B) 2
C) 3
D) 4

4) Did Tom Kelly win his last-ever regular-season game as a Twins' manager?

A) Yes
B) No

5) What are the most wins by a Twins' pitcher in a single season?

    A) 34
    B) 35
    C) 36
    D) 37

6) Who holds the Twins' record for the most doubles in a season?

    A) Sam Rice
    B) Mickey Vernon
    C) Justin Morneau
    D) Delmon Young

7) Who is the most recent Twins' pitcher to strike out four players in a single inning?

    A) Walter Johnson
    B) Johan Santana
    C) Jim Kaat
    D) Scott Baker

8) Minnesota has more pitchers than outfielders enshrined in the National Baseball Hall of Fame.

    A) True
    B) False

9) Against whom did Gene Larkin hit his single for a walk-off run in Game Seven of the 1991 World Series?

    A) Tom Glavine
    B) Mike Stanton
    C) John Smoltz
    D) Alejandro Peña

10) What is the Twins' record for the most runs scored in a nine-inning game?

    A) 24
    B) 25
    C) 26
    D) 27

1) B – 2 (Bucky Harris [1924] and Tom Kelly [1987 and 1991])

2) C – 7 (Game One in 1924, Games Two and Six in 1925, Games Four and Five in 1933 and Games Three and Four in 1991)

3) B – 2 (Tim Belcher, drafted No. 1 overall in 1983, refused to sign with the Twins. The Twins also drafted Joe Mauer as No. 1 overall in 2001.)

4) A – Yes (The Twins defeated the Chicago White Sox, 8-5, in his final game as manager.)

5) C – 36 (Walter Johnson led the American League in 1913.)

6) B – Mickey Vernon (51 doubles in 1946 [led the league])

7) D – Scott Baker (This took place in the third inning at a game against the Milwaukee Brewers on June 15, 2008.)

8) B – False (Only two Twins' pitchers [Walter Johnson and Bert Blyleven] have been inducted, whereas six Twins' outfielders have been.)

9) D – Alejandro Peña (Mike Stanton was injured in the ninth inning. Peña pitched in the tenth inning, loaded the bases, giving Larkin a chance to win the game.)

10) A – 24 (The Twins beat the Detroit Tigers, 24-11, on April 24, 1996.)

Note: All answers valid as of the end of the 2010 season, unless otherwise indicated in the question itself.

Player / Team Score Sheet

Name:_____

Spring Training			Regular Season			Postseason			Championship Series			Extra Innings Bonus	
1		26		1		26		1		26		1		26		1	
2		27		2		27		2		27		2		27		2	
3		28		3		28		3		28		3		28		3	
4		29		4		29		4		29		4		29		4	
5		30		5		30		5		30		5		30		5	
6		31		6		31		6		31		6		31		6	
7		32		7		32		7		32		7		32		7	
8		33		8		33		8		33		8		33		8	
9		34		9		34		9		34		9		34		9	
10		35		10		35		10		35		10		35		10	
11		36		11		36		11		36		11		36			
12		37		12		37		12		37		12		37			
13		38		13		38		13		38		13		38			
14		39		14		39		14		39		14		39			
15		40		15		40		15		40		15		40			
16		41		16		41		16		41		16		41			
17		42		17		42		17		42		17		42			
18		43		18		43		18		43		18		43			
19		44		19		44		19		44		19		44			
20		45		20		45		20		45		20		45			
21		46		21		46		21		46		21		46			
22		47		22		47		22		47		22		47			
23		48		23		48		23		48		23		48			
24		49		24		49		24		49		24		49			
25		50		25		50		25		50		25		50			
___ x 1 =___			___ x 2 =___			___ x 3 =___			___ x 4 =___			___ x 4 =___	

Multiply total number correct by point value/quarter to calculate totals for each quarter.

Add total of all quarters below.

Total Points:_____

Thank you for playing *Twinsology Trivia Challenge*.

Additional score sheets are available at:
www.TriviaGameBooks.com

Player / Team Score Sheet

Name:_____

Spring Training		Regular Season		Postseason		Championship Series		Extra Innings Bonus	
1		26	1		26	1		26	1		26	1	
2		27	2		27	2		27	2		27	2	
3		28	3		28	3		28	3		28	3	
4		29	4		29	4		29	4		29	4	
5		30	5		30	5		30	5		30	5	
6		31	6		31	6		31	6		31	6	
7		32	7		32	7		32	7		32	7	
8		33	8		33	8		33	8		33	8	
9		34	9		34	9		34	9		34	9	
10		35	10		35	10		35	10		35	10	
11		36	11		36	11		36	11		36		
12		37	12		37	12		37	12		37		
13		38	13		38	13		38	13		38		
14		39	14		39	14		39	14		39		
15		40	15		40	15		40	15		40		
16		41	16		41	16		41	16		41		
17		42	17		42	17		42	17		42		
18		43	18		43	18		43	18		43		
19		44	19		44	19		44	19		44		
20		45	20		45	20		45	20		45		
21		46	21		46	21		46	21		46		
22		47	22		47	22		47	22		47		
23		48	23		48	23		48	23		48		
24		49	24		49	24		49	24		49		
25		50	25		50	25		50	25		50		

____ x 1 =____ ____ x 2 =____ ____ x 3 =____ ____ x 4 =____ ____ x 4 =____

Multiply total number correct by point value/quarter to calculate totals for each quarter.

Add total of all quarters below.

Total Points:_____

Thank you for playing *Twinsology Trivia Challenge*.

Additional score sheets are available at:
www.TriviaGameBooks.com